# Simply Pickles

## A LITTLE BOOK OF TEMPTING CHUTNEYS, PRESERVES AND RELISHES

### SARA RIDGLEY

ILLUSTRATIONS BY MADELEINE DAVID

GRUB STREET · LONDON

Published by Grub Street
The Basement, 10 Chivalry Road, London SW11 1HT

Copyright © Grub Street 1995
Text copyright © Sara Ridgley 1995
Illustrations copyright © Madeleine David

**British Library Cataloguing in Publication Data**
Ridgley, Sara
Simply Pickles
I. Title
641.8
ISBN 1-898697-23-X

Printed and bound in Spain by Graficas Reunidas

# CHILLI WARNING

*This is to remind you to take care when preparing fresh chillies.
Use a fork or tongs to hold the chilli or wear disposable plastic gloves.
Wash the knife and board carefully and never touch your face or rub
your eyes while preparing them.*

# STORAGE

*All pickle storage jars need vinegar-proof lids. Glass, plastic or
plastic-coated lids are fine, but unprotected metal coverings will
deteriorate rapidly. Label the jars (unless you really like surprises)
and store in a cool, dark place for the best results.*

# CONTENTS

# FOREWORD

When I was small, the phrase 'You little pickle' was often applied to me. Can't think why. But it seems to have stuck. I am now known locally as Mrs Pickle, Sara the Pickle, or even the Pickled Lady. This last one I deny.

Anyone looking for me just follows the smell of vinegar and spices. In my kitchen you will find me, glasses misted up, mumbling 'Hubble Bubble, Toil and Trouble' over a steaming vat of fragrant chutney. Labels and ladles at the ready, I'm very happy amongst my apricots and apples, sultanas and cinnamon. Bunches of fresh herbs for salad dressings stand to attention. Shall I make Dracula's Dread or Lucifer's Soup today? Baskets of furiously fiery chillies, home grown tomatoes, crunchy onions and juicy garlic wait their turn. The aromas of zesty fresh ginger, lemons, peaches and honey, mustard seeds and muscavado waft out of the kitchen window. In the old days, I'd probably have been hot favourite for the ducking stool.

The neighbours seem to be used to it.

'Aha,' I hear them say, 'Smells like Sticky Peach chutney today. Might be Zingy Lemon? Could do with a jar of that. I've got some empties for Sara anyway.'

Round they come, fighting their way through the vinegar fumes, bearing gifts of empty jars. In summer, I disappear under armfuls of excess runner beans, marrows the size of narrowboats and carrier bags of courgettes. Now's the time for my Mediterranean chutney. Out comes the Chillililli recipe. My hands turn a deep shade of cerise from peeling beetroot and slicing red cabbage. Better get started on the pickled onions. My husband comes home to a red-eyed, red-handed woman who reeks of pickled eggs. I wonder if he'd like me to get a proper job?

I am probably the worst person in the world to be writing a

recipe book. I never follow recipes. I start with a vague idea and one ingredient, then add other bits and pieces with gay abandon. Sometimes things definitely don't turn out as I'd hoped. Sometimes the end result is delicious. And when that's the case, it's always the one I didn't write down. So I start all over again to recreate it, making notes this time.

Some of these recipes have turned up in my brain at 3 o'clock in the morning when I've been wondering what on earth to do with 35 pounds of green tomatoes. Others have materialised because I haven't been able to find anything in the shops with the right levels of heat, jazz and spice for my tastebuds. Hellish Relish is one of these. The combination of chillies, garlic, onions and ginger is dazzlingly hot. Bangkok Blaster dressing was the result of an evening in a Thai restaurant, enjoying one of their outstanding dips and returning home at midnight to concoct a chilli dressing to recreate the flavours I'd tasted earlier. The kitchen echoed with cries of:

'Nearly, nearly. Needs a bit more ginger...' *and*
'Could you pass the fire extinguisher, please? Overdid the chillies.' *and finally*
'Yes, that's exactly it!'

So, if you enjoy playing Chemistry Professors in your kitchen and experimenting with flavours, textures and colours, have a bash at some of my favourites. Naturally, all the ingredients are listed and amounts are usually specified but I find the chilli/garlic/spice intensity levels are a very personal matter. I have made Swearbox Sambal that has left my lips numb after half a teaspoonful and my husband lying on the floor in shock, whilst others eat half a jar and, ignoring the steam coming out of their ears, comment:

'Huh, it's not THAT hot. Honestly.'

These people are either brave or batty. Do join us....

Sara Ridgley

# HELLISH RELISH

*Lucifer could have invented this! Steam may come out of your ears ...*

## INGREDIENTS

| | |
|---|---|
| 4 tbs | Onion, chopped |
| 2 tbs | Garlic, chopped |
| 2 tbs | Ginger, chopped |
| 4 | Fresh red chillies, sliced |
| | Raspberry vinegar |
| 1 tbs | Caster sugar |
| 1 tsp | Chinese seasoning |

## CHEF'S TIP

*Leave the chillies out for not-quite-so Hellish Relish. White wine vinegar can replace Raspberry Vinegar, but add a teaspoon of honey as well.*

## METHOD

Alternate layers of onion, garlic, ginger and chillies in a small, wide-necked jar. Shake up the vinegar with the sugar and seasonings and pour it over. Safe to use after a couple of days, depending on your level of courage - but do be brave enough before six months.

## USES

*For a flavour-studded side-dish to accompany Asian food, add a couple of teaspoons to a bowl of fresh pineapple pieces. Mango, orange or pawpaw make an interesting alternative. Added to stir fried prawns or chicken, it will lend a devilish dimension to the menu. Mixed with a little olive oil it will pep up a simple salad of celery, cucumber and crispy lettuce.*

Makes about 200ml (7 fl oz).

# SPECIAL RESERVE

*Christmas is its middle name. Succulent sherry-soaked fruit with irresistible flavour - just open the jar and throw the lid away, because once you start ....*

## INGREDIENTS

Your choice of:    Dried apricots
Sultanas
Glacé cherries
Dried pears
Dried peaches
Raisins
Dried pineapple
Dried pawpaw
Dates
Mixed peel
Pale cream sherry

## CHEF'S TIP

*Use dry sherry if you prefer. Also marvellous made with a dessert wine, brandy or non-sparkling apple juice.*

## METHOD

Cram a selection of interesting small jars with layers of your favourite dried fruits and simply fill with sherry to cover the fruit generously.
Top up the jars next morning because the fruit will drink the sherry during the night. What could be easier than this recipe? The hardest part is leaving it for 48 hours before you open the jar and devour the delights inside! For masochists, it will keep several years.

## USES

*Make pretty material tops for your jars and give them as gifts. You'll be the most popular person in the district. Use it in a sponge cake,*

steamed pudding, malt loaf, fruit cake or scones and relish the
richness. Sensational on ice cream. A good friend of mine uses hers to
make fruity sweet dumplings, combining the remaining sherry with
orange juice and honey as a memorable sauce. Use the drunken fruit
in a moist stuffing for the turkey, adding the sherry to the gravy.
Excellent as a sauce for gammon or pork steaks. Add it to a risotto,
chicken casserole .... I'll leave it to your imagination.

Makes as much as you can store.

# SPICED GINGER

*Hot, sweet, salty and spicy, this aromatic, appealing condiment is
China, compressed.*

| INGREDIENTS | |
|---|---|
| 1 tbs | Sesame oil |
| 250g (8 oz) | Fresh peeled ginger, cut into chunks |
| 1 tbs | Cinnamon |
| 1 tbs | Nutmeg |
| 1 tbs | Coriander seeds, crushed |
| 1 tbs | Mace |
| 1 tsp | Black pepper |
| 1 tbs | Soy sauce |
| 150ml (¼ pt) | Sherry |
| 300ml (¼ pt) | Sherry vinegar |
| 4 tbs | Honey |
| 4 tbs | Muscovado sugar |

| CHEF'S TIP |
|---|

*Effective with ginger shreds instead of chunks. Perfectly wonderful
sugar-free, the spices lend sweetness on their own.*

## METHOD

Heat the sesame oil in a wok, add the ginger and stir fry for one minute. Add the spices and stir fry for one minute. Add the soy sauce, sherry, vinegar and honey. Stir fry for another minute. Add the sugar. Stir until it has dissolved. Turn up the heat and cook until the liquid is reduced by half. Pour into small jars. Keep for a week (if you can) before sampling. Believe it or not, it will keep a good year or more.

## USES

*Imagine the scene. An exclusive restaurant high in the hills of Szechuan. A waiter presents a whole lobster on a silver platter. Bamboo baskets of steamed dim sum decorate the table. Peking Duck waits to be devoured. What? No Spiced Ginger? That's it then, we're off.... Even if it's only a Chinese take-away, this recipe does marvels for pancake rolls, prawn chow mein or anything with egg in it. A good friend, Cindy Bishop, insists it cured her bronchitis when all else failed. The Chinese tell us that ginger is a powerful healer - who are we to argue? Little jars make terrific Christmas gifts.*

Makes three 125g
(4 oz) jars.

# RED CABBAGE

*Traditional, spiced or fruited red cabbage complements any cold collation.*

TRADITIONAL RED CABBAGE INGREDIENTS

| 1 | Hard red cabbage |
|---|---|
| | Salt |
| | Pepper |
| | Muscovado sugar |
| | Red wine vinegar |

## SPICED RED CABBAGE INGREDIENTS

| 1 Quantity | Traditional red cabbage |
|---|---|
| 4 | Dried red chillies, crushed |
| 3 | Garlic cloves |
| 1 tsp | Coriander seeds |
| 1 tsp | Cloves |
| 1 tsp | Cardamom pods |
| 1 tbs | Mustard seeds |

## FRUITED RED CABBAGE INGREDIENTS

| 1 Quantity | Traditional red cabbage |
|---|---|
| 125g (4 oz) | Sultanas |
| 125g (4 oz) | Dried apricots |
| 2 | Dessert apples, chopped |

### CHEF'S TIP

*For Spiced and Fruited Cabbage, combine the two recipes. Cut the cabbage into mixed slices and chunks. Thick bits stay crunchy longer.*

### METHOD

Pack the chopped cabbage into jars. Add seasonings and sugar to taste. For Spiced Cabbage, sprinkle the spices in as you fill the jars. For Fruited Cabbage, intersperse fruit with cabbage. Fill jars with vinegar. Vinegar will be absorbed overnight so top up the jars before storing in a dark place. Start eating in 2 days. Keeps for 3 months.

### USES

*Lends a splash of colour to a buffet or Ploughmans. Add a sliced onion or cauliflower florets to each jar - pink onion rings look great on chicken salad. Served hot, it's perfect with pork, especially Fruited. Make it with granulated sweetener for a virtually calorie-free snack. Traditional with Lancashire hot pot, it also suits Shepherd's Pie.*

Makes about five 500g (1 lb) jars.

# APRICOT, ONION AND GINGER CHUTNEY

*Frightfully fruity, packed with the richness of apricots and the contrasting savoury crunch of onion, this chutney is warm and zesty, courtesy of our old friend, ginger.*

## INGREDIENTS

| | |
|---|---|
| 500g (1 lb) | Dried apricots |
| Juice of 2 | Oranges |
| 1 tsp | White pepper |
| 2 tsp | Ground ginger |
| 3 | Onions, chopped |
| 2 tsp | Salt |
| 2 tbs | Fresh ginger, chopped |
| 2 tbs | Honey |
| 3 tbs | Demerara sugar |
| 600ml (1 pt) | Cider vinegar |

## CHEF'S TIP

*An economical way to buy apricots is to ask your healthfood shop for apricot pieces.*

## METHOD

Soak the apricots overnight in 300ml (½ pt) water mixed with the orange juice. Put everything except the sugar and vinegar in a large pan or wok and bubble it for an hour, stirring frequently. Add the sugar and vinegar. Cook for about a further hour till the foam disappears from the top of the chutney to leave a glossy finish and the

chutney 'draws' in the wake of a wooden spoon pulled across the pan. Ready now or will store for at least a year.

## USES

*A real cracker with curry, this chutney goes well with rich dishes like Lamb Passanda and Chicken Tikka Masala. Also complements vegetable courses, especially onion or mushroom bhajis and potato with spinach. Good with rice, particularly birianis and terrific with tandoori chicken. A wonderful accompaniment for pork tenderloin or crown of lamb. Use it as a glaze for a pair of roast poussin, then add a little cream and extra chutney to the pan juices for a delicately fruity sauce. A natural partner for Wensleydale, Smoked Galloway or Caerphilly.*

Makes about three 500g (1 lb) jars.

# AUBERGINES ROSA

*A fabulously fragrant pickle with Italian blood in its veins. Delicious on its own, washed down by a goblet of Barolo.*

## INGREDIENTS

| | |
|---|---|
| 6 small | Aubergines, trimmed and sliced into rounds |
| 6 cloves | Garlic, peeled and sliced |
| 1 small | Red pepper, sliced into rounds |
| 2 tsp | Dried oregano |
| 2 tsp | Dried thyme |
| 1 tsp | Garlic salt |
| 1 tsp | Coarsely ground black pepper |

| | |
|---|---|
| 1 tsp | Honey |
| 3 tbs | Olive oil |
| 300ml (½ pt) | Red wine |
| 300ml (½ pt) | Red wine vinegar |

## CHEF'S TIP

*Some like it hot! Add a chopped red chilli if you do.*

## METHOD

Heat 1 tablespoonful of olive oil in a pan and fry the aubergines, garlic and red pepper for two minutes. Spoon them into wide-necked jars, sprinkling in the herbs and seasonings. Mix the honey with the red wine and pour it in. Top up with vinegar and finally, a sealing layer of olive oil. Store in a dark cupboard for two weeks before breaking open this luscious, "meaty" pickle. Won't keep longer than about four months but you'll probably consume it in a week anyway!

## USES

*Pick a sunny Sunday. Invite a few friends round. Open the Valpolicella, put Pavarotti on to sing and the pasta on to boil. Fill a basket with chunks of warm Ciabata bread and make an antipasti platter of Aubergines Rosa, Parma ham, black and green olives, sun-dried tomatoes and mushrooms in herb oil. They'll be clamouring for more Aubergines Rosa to accompany the Dolcelatte. Serve on the side with a sage and onion omelette for a light supper.*

Makes about four 500g (1lb) jars.

# CHILILILILLI

*Strong nerves are required to eat this pickle. Make it as hot as you like but issue a public warning when you serve it up!*

## INGREDIENTS

| | |
|---|---|
| 5 | Fresh green or red chillies, finely sliced |
| 250g (8 oz) | Marrow/courgette/cucumber, chopped |
| 175g (6 oz) | Cauliflower florets |
| 125g (4 oz) | Silverskin onions |
| 1 | Red pepper, diced |
| 1 | Carrot, diced |
| 5 cloves | Garlic, crushed |
| 1 tbs | Fresh ginger, finely chopped |
| 900ml (1½ pt) | Malt vinegar |
| | Garlic salt and black pepper |
| 1 tbs | Crushed dried red chillies |
| 2 tbs | Demerara sugar |
| 1 tbs | Mustard seeds |
| 1 tbs | Ground ginger |
| 2 tbs | Turmeric |
| 1 tbs | Chilli powder |
| 3 tbs | Mustard powder |
| 2 tbs | Cornflour |

## CHEF'S TIP

*Don't overcook the vegetables, they should be crunchy, not soft. Use ordinary onions, chopped, if silverskins are difficult to obtain.*

## METHOD

Cook the chopped vegetables for three minutes in most of the vinegar, salt and pepper. Add the dried chillies, sugar and mustard seeds. Mix the ginger, turmeric, chilli and mustard powders to a paste with half the remaining vinegar. Add to the pot. Cook for two minutes more. Mix the cornflour and last of the vinegar to a paste. Add the cornflour carefully, stirring until you have a thickish, bright yellow mixture flecked with red and green. Get it into jars before it makes an escape bid. You can eat it now but the longer you leave it in the jar, the hotter it becomes.

*I know a man who reckons Chillililli is 'the business' with cold lamb sandwiches. Me, I'm not so sure, but it is excellent with salami, sausage rolls or ham. Blue cheeses wear it well. The longer you leave it in the jar, the hotter it gets. Stand by for breaking glass.*

Makes about four 500g (1 lb) jars.

# HONION CHUTNEY

*A sweet and succulent chutney with spicy overtones and inviting fruitiness.*

## INGREDIENTS

| | |
|---|---|
| 8 large | Onions, peeled and chopped |
| 6 tbs | Honey |
| 300g (10 oz) | Sultanas |
| 2 | Eating apples, peeled, cored and chopped |
| 600ml (1 pt) | Cider vinegar |
| 2 tbs | French mustard |
| 1 tbs | Cinnamon |
| 1 tbs | Ground ginger |
| 1 tsp | Salt |

## CHEF'S TIP

*Try replacing the cinnamon with nutmeg or ground coriander.*

## METHOD

Cook everything except the spices and mustard in a

large pan until the mixture feels sticky.  Stir in the mustard and spices and cook for 15 minutes more until the chutney 'draws' darkly across the pan.  Jar and store in a dark place for a minimum of a month. Still tastes fabulous a year later when fully matured.

*Find the strongest Cheddar you can and settle down with a cheering chunk of it, a crusty handful of Ciabata bread, a dozen cherry tomatoes and a serious spoonful of this chutney.  Or try a different cheese - Shropshire Blue, Dorset Vinney or St Paulin.  Replace the cheese with a platter of cold pork or beef and you'll soon find out how well Honion complements meat.  Try it in a cold turkey sandwich.  Perfect with pork pie, herby sausage plait or quiche.  Great as a glaze on a roasting leg of lamb.*

Makes about five 500g (1 lb) jars.

# CHISTMAS CHUTNEY WITH SHERRY

*A rich and tempting chutney.  One spoonful and visions of a succulent slice of Christmas pudding with brandy butter float before your eyes…*

## INGREDIENTS

| | |
|---|---|
| 250g  (8 oz) | Sultanas |
| 250g  (8 oz) | Raisins |
| 125g  (4 oz) | Dried apricots |
| 125g  (4 oz) | Chopped dates |
| 600ml (1 pt) | Cream sherry |
| 250g  (8 oz) | Apples, chopped |
| 125g  (4 oz) | Onions, chopped |
| 1 can | Crushed pineapple |
| | Rind and juice of 1 Orange |

| Juice of | 1 Lemon |
|---|---|
| 1 tsp | Nutmeg |
| 1 tsp | Cinnamon |
| 900ml (1½ pt) | Malt vinegar |
| | Salt, Pepper |
| 500g (1 lb) | Muscovado sugar |
| 2 tbs | Black treacle |
| 50g (2 oz) | Glacé cherries |
| 50g (2 oz) | Crystallised ginger |

## METHOD

Soak the sultanas, raisins, apricots and dates in sherry for two hours. Spoon the drunken dried fruit into a large pan with the apple, onions, pineapple, orange and lemon juice, more sherry and 300ml (½ pt) water. Cook for half an hour then add the spices, vinegar, salt, pepper, sugar and treacle. Bubble for another hour, stirring well to prevent sticking, then add the orange peel, cherries, ginger and remaining sherry. Ten more minutes will produce a glossy chutney which 'draws' when you pull a wooden spoon across the pan. Bottle it hot. Cut out pretty Christmassy tops from fabric scraps or wrapping paper to dress up the lids. Add a touch of ribbon - presents to go! Enjoy this chutney straight away or store until next Christmas - it keeps well.

## USES

*Cold turkey or pork beg for this chutney and you must serve it with your Christmas ham and cheeseboard or they'll write to Santa and complain. Ideal with a good strong blue such as Roquefort or Stilton, its richness has a wedge of game pie or onion quiche in raptures. Try it with roast chicken instead of redcurrant jelly. Mix a tablespoonful with a glass of sherry or port and add it to the roasting tin for a seasonal Cumberland sauce-type gravy. Ho-ho-ho!*

Makes about seven 500g (1 lb) jars.

# FIGS FRAGOULIS

*A sun-ripe succulent relish, crying out for Feta cheese, chilled Retsina, olive oil bread and a stunning sea view. I'll send you a postcard...!*

## INGREDIENTS

| | |
|---|---|
| 6 | Ripe figs |
| 30 | Black olives |
| 1 | Red onion, quartered |
| 5 tbs | Olive oil |
| 5 tbs | Red wine vinegar |
| 2 tbs | Runny honey |
| A scrunch | Sea salt and black pepper |
| 6 | Fresh basil leaves |

## CHEF'S TIP

*Fly to the Ionian islands to make this dish. You can buy the ingredients at the right price and the sunshine makes all the difference ...*

Cut open the figs, scoop out the juicy, seedy fruit and discard the skins. Mix chunks of fig with the olives and onion and place in a shallow dish. Stir the olive oil and red wine vinegar into the honey, add the salt and pepper and pour it over the fig mixture. Garnish with fresh basil. Can also be made in advance and stored in jars for up to a week - don't add the basil until serving time.

**U S E S**

*A wonderful accompaniment for Greek food, especially grilled or barbecued meats. Lamb souvlaki, grilled liver with orange and chicken and red pepper kebabs all appreciate Figs Fragoulis. Great with grilled fish, particularly swordfish steaks or juicy giant prawns. A simple salad with chunks of crumbly Feta cheese and cool cucumber, Figs Fragoulis is also outstanding rolled inside thin slices of wind-dried ham or crisp Cos lettuce leaves.*

Makes approx 600g (1¼ lb)

# NUTCASE CHUTNEY

*Juicy fruits and a crunchy cornucopia of nuts make this rich chutney deliciously different.*

**I N G R E D I E N T S**

| | |
|---|---|
| 125g (4 oz) | Dried apricots |
| 250g (8 oz) | Sultanas |
| 250g (8 oz) | Raisins |
| 250g (8 oz) | Dates |
| 300ml (½ pt) | Apple juice |
| 250g (8 oz) | Apples |
| 250g (8 oz) | Onions |

| | |
|---|---|
| 250g (8 oz) | Carrots |
| 125g (4 oz) | Cashew nuts |
| 125g (4 oz) | Hazelnuts |
| 125g (4 oz) | Brazil nuts |
| Good grating | Nutmeg |
| 2 tsp | Cinnamon |
| 1.2 litres (2 pt) | Malt vinegar |
| 1 tsp | Salt |
| 1 tsp | Black pepper |
| 2 tbs | Black treacle |
| 500g (1 lb) | Muscovado sugar |

## METHOD

Soak the apricots, dates, sultanas and raisins in the apple juice for two hours. Put all the fruit, vegetables and nuts in a large pan with the spices, vinegar and remaining apple juice. Cook for 30 minutes. Add the salt, pepper, treacle and sugar and cook for about 1 hour until the chutney is glossy and 'draws' across the bottom of the pan. Ready now or will keep at least a year.

## USES

*The perfect partner for cheeses, especially full-flavoured farmhouse Cheddar, ripe Stilton or a good strong blue. Experiment with something offbeat like Dorset Vinney or Blue Cheshire. A crunchy accompaniment to a thick slice of cold pork or roast beef, especially with leftover boiled potatoes fried in a little olive oil with a shot of Dracula's Dread dressing (page 48) and a handful of chopped shallots. Wonderful with gala pie or duck paté.*
*A popular Christmas chutney, its moist richness goes well with turkey.*

Makes about
six 500g
(1 lb) jars.

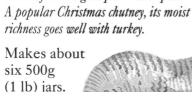

# FRUITBOWL CHUTNEY

*A luscious, appetising chutney, dark, rich and bursting with plump fruit.*

| | |
|---|---|
| 250g (8 oz) | Dried apricots |
| 125g (4 oz) | Dried pawpaw |
| 125g (4 oz) | Sultanas |
| 125g (4 oz) | Raisins |
| 175g (6 oz) | Dates, chopped |
| Juice of 1 | Orange |
| 1 tbs | Cinnamon |
| 300ml ($\frac{1}{2}$ pt) | Port |
| 2 large | Apples, chopped |
| 2 large | Onions, chopped |
| 2 tbs | Black treacle |
| 500g (1 lb) | Muscovado sugar |
| 900ml ($1\frac{1}{2}$ pt) | Malt vinegar |
| | Salt |
| | Black pepper |

## METHOD

Soak the apricots, pawpaw, sultanas, raisins and dates for two hours in the orange juice, cinnamon and port. Add the remaining ingredients and cook for about $1\frac{1}{2}$ hours, adding more juice (or port) if anything dares to stick. Bubble till the chutney is glossy. Bottle it in chunky jars. Makes an original and interesting gift. Tastes just as good this Christmas season as it will next.

## USES

*A really festive chutney. Imagine it's Boxing Day teatime. You're plastering a length of crusty French bread with real butter (well, it IS*

*Christmas), adding a wedge of mature cheddar and a generous spoonful of chutney, a slice of home-cooked gammon or turkey breast and a hot pickled onion or three. Makes the mouth water, doesn't it? I can hear the log fire crackling already. Also a perfect partner for a wedge of game pie, a flaky pastry sausage roll or a quarter of quiche - its sweet, tangy richness sets off savouries a treat.*

Makes about five 500g (1 lb) jars.

# PRUNES PALAZZO

*An unusual tracklement to perk up paté and add an invigorating slant to the cheeseboard.*

## INGREDIENTS

| | |
|---|---|
| 250g (8oz) | Dried prunes |
| Juice of 1 | Orange |
| 300ml (½ pt) | Pale cream sherry |
| 3 | Garlic cloves, peeled and sliced |
| 1 | Orange, sliced |
| 6 sprigs | Fresh oregano |
| 1 tbs | Light soy sauce |
| 150ml (¼ pt) | Sherry vinegar |
| 1 tsp | Ground black pepper |
| | Olive oil |

## CHEF'S TIP

*A sprinkling of cloves makes an interesting addition. Try replacing half the prunes with dried apricots.*

## METHOD

Soak the prunes overnight in the orange juice and sherry. Layer the prunes with the garlic, orange slices and herb sprigs in attractive jars. Add the soy sauce, sherry vinegar and pepper and top up with olive oil. I use more oil than vinegar in this recipe, but it's all a matter of personal choice. Experiment! Keep for 3 days before using this different condiment. If you had an iron will, it would keep for up to a month.

## USES

*Spoon a prune or two on to a platter of ripe cheeses. What a combination! Brie, Camembert and Smoked Bavarian will appeal to mild-taste fans and Roquefort, Feta and Stilton really tingle on the palate when enjoyed with Prunes Palazzo. Intriguing with robust*

*terrines, especially duck and pork, this relish will also be appreciated
with salami, bresaola and Parma ham. Try adding to a rabbit
casserole or roast lamb.*

Makes about two 500g (1lb) jars.

# HOT CORN RELISH

*Break out the burgers, here comes the Hot Corn. Crunchy and savoury,
a hot - but not hellish - relish.*

## INGREDIENTS

| | |
|---|---|
| 500g (1 lb) | Sweetcorn |
| 1 tsp | Mixed herbs |
| 1 tsp | Salt |
| 1 tsp | Black pepper |
| 1 tsp | Mustard |
| 1 tsp | Ground ginger |
| 2 tsp | Chilli powder |
| 1 carton | Passata |
| 250g (8 oz) | Tomatoes, liquidized |
| 4 | Onions, chopped |
| 4 | Green chillies, chopped |
| 3 tbs | Demerara sugar |
| 600ml (1 pt) | Red wine vinegar |

## CHEF'S TIP

*If you're not keen on sweetcorn, replace it with chopped butter beans,
celery, apple or even carrot.*

## METHOD

Pile everything into a big pan and cook it for 45
minutes until it's thick and spreadable, then jar it.
Can be used immediately or made on a cold April day

in anticipation of barbecues to come in the summer. Will keep about a year.

*A great barbecue relish, complementing sausages, steaks, chops and especially burgers in buns. Equally interesting with fish. Try spreading it on a sheet of foil, topping it with a cod or haddock steak and smearing the fish with extra relish. Squeeze a lemon over the fish, fasten the parcel and cook it gently in the oven or over the cool part of the barbecue. Adds a distinct zap to a pan of tomato soup or a chicken casserole. Serve it with onion tart or add it to a soft cream cheese for dips and dunks.*

Makes about four 500g (1 lb) jars.

# PICALILLI

*Mustardy and mouthwatering. Fresh vegetables from the garden or the market lend this pickle its classic crunch - and it's quick to cook.*

## INGREDIENTS

| | |
|---|---|
| 175g (6 oz) | Cauliflower florets |
| 125g (4 oz) | Onions, chopped |
| 900ml (1½ pt) | Malt vinegar |
| 1 tsp | Salt |
| 1 tsp | Pepper |
| 1 tsp | Mustard seeds |
| 2 tbs | Demerara sugar |
| 250g (8 oz) | Mixed marrow/courgettes/cucumber, chopped |
| 1 tbs | Turmeric |
| 1 tbs | Ground ginger |

| | |
|---|---|
| 1 tbs | Mustard powder |
| 2 tbs | Cornflour |

## CHEF'S TIP

*For a rich colour and extra tang, add a tablespoon of tomato purée after the first five minutes cooking. If courgettes are expensive, replace with carrots.*

## METHOD

Cook the cauliflower and onions in most of the vinegar, salt and pepper for 5 minutes. Add the mustard seeds, sugar and remaining vegetables. Make a thin paste of the turmeric, ginger and mustard powder with half the remaining vinegar and add to the vegetables. Cook for two minutes. Blend the cornflour with the rest of the vinegar. Add gradually to the pan, stirring constantly as it starts to thicken. When you have the required consistency, turn off the heat and bottle straightaway. You can eat it now - my husband won't even wait for it to cool, but it will keep for at least a year. One lady I know unearths the same jar every Christmas and enjoys a few spoonfuls. The Picalilli is five years old and still tastes wonderful, apparently!

## USES

*A popular accompaniment for crumbly cheese or succulent ham, this is also terrific with salads or in a cold pork sandwich. Excellent with Scotch eggs. Different as a dip with celery sticks or tortilla chips. Gives a plain omelette the edge and livens up cold chicken. A useful chutney to make whenever you have a glut of vegetables.*

Makes abour four 500g (1 lb) jars.

# MEDITERRANEAN CHUTNEY

*Tomatoes, courgettes, onions and garlic bring back memories of Greek, Spanish and Italian meals enjoyed on a shady terrace overlooking a sparkling sea. A chunky, ratatouille-style chutney. Sunshine in a jar!*

## INGREDIENTS

| | |
|---|---|
| 4 | Courgettes |
| 10 | Garlic cloves |
| 4 | Onions |
| 12 large | Tomatoes |
| 150ml ($\frac{1}{4}$ pt) | Red wine |
| 1 tsp | Salt |
| 1 tsp | Black pepper |
| 2 tbs | Tomato purée |
| 2 tbs | Olive oil |
| 300ml ($\frac{1}{2}$ pt) | Red wine vinegar |
| Juice of 1 | Lemon |
| 2 tbs | Honey |
| 2 tsp | Fresh rosemary |
| 2 tsp | Fresh sage |
| 2 tsp | Fresh thyme |
| 2 tsp | Fresh oregano |
| 2 tsp | Fresh basil |

## CHEF'S TIP

*A tablespoonful of chopped black or green olives makes an interesting addition.*

## METHOD

Chop the vegetables and poach in red wine for 20 minutes. Add the salt and pepper, tomato purée, oil, vinegar and lemon juice. Cook for 10 minutes. Add the honey and herbs (except the basil) and the olives,

if you're using them. Cook for 5 minutes more then add the basil. Jar it straightaway. This chutney is ready now and won't keep for ever (2-3 months) but it's so delicious, it will disappear in no time anyway!

## USES

*Great with grilled lamb. Resurrect those holiday flavours by serving with swordfish steaks or fresh sardines sprinkled with thyme and olive oil and sizzled under the grill. Marinate chicken breasts in a tablespoonful mixed with red wine. Add to a tuna casserole for that Italian flavour. A dollop drives an omelette dotty and suits sausages a treat. For an ultra-fast healthy meal, try a tablespoonful on a helping of wholewheat pasta. Interesting mixed with saffron rice, topped with an optional fried egg!*

Makes six 500g (1 lb) jars.

# PUNCHY PINEAPPLE RELISH

*A jazzy, fiery, fruity tracklement to dazzle the tastebuds. Mouthwatering with rich morsels like dim sum or salt-baked king prawns. And an extra bonus - no cooking involved.*

## INGREDIENTS

| | |
|---|---|
| 1 | Large fresh pineapple |
| 250g (8 oz) | Shallots |
| 6 | Red chillies |
| 1 tbs | Black peppercorns |
| | Sea salt |
| | Caster sugar or clear honey |

Prepare the pineapple and chop it into bite-sized chunks. Peel the shallots and slice them in half across the middle, not end to end. Slice the chillies diagonally. Use the seeds if you want it really hot, leave them out if not. Pack the pineapple into jars with the shallots placed to show off their ringed pattern. Intersperse with the chilli pieces and peppercorns. Allow a large pinch of salt and two teaspoonfuls of caster sugar or honey per 500g (1 lb) jar. Top up with vinegar and give each jar a good shake. Store for three days before using. Keeps for at least two months.

## USES

*A refreshing relish with Malaysian or Chinese food, especially pork dumplings, spring rolls or fish. Why not add a few fresh strawberries for a really unusual effect? Definitely different with a farmhouse Cheddar or Ploughmans Lunch with ham. Makes a larynx-tickling addition to sweet and sour sauce or a stir-fry. Jazzes up rice and cheers up a curry. Adds an exotic touch to a lamb hotpot. Serve with crispy haddock chunks fried in a light batter made from whipped egg white, cornflour and sherry. Scrumptious!*

Makes about three 500g (1 lb) jars.

# MARATHON CHUTNEY

*A delicious green delight - and an excellent way to preserve those excess vegetables.*

| | |
|---|---|
| 1 kg (2 lb) | Runner or French beans |
| 500g (1 1b) | Green tomatoes |
| 500g (1 lb) | Cooking apples |
| 500g (1 lb) | Onions |
| 500g (1 lb) | Caster sugar |
| 10 | Garlic cloves |
| Walnut-sized piece | Fresh ginger, peeled |
| 1.2 litres (2 pt) | Cider vinegar |
| 300ml (½ pt) | Crabbies Green Ginger Wine |
| Juice of 1 | Lime |
| 1 tbs | Ground coriander |
| Large bunch | Fresh coriander |
| Large bunch | Fresh basil |

## CHEF'S TIP

*Add a couple of chopped green chillies to this mouthwatering mix - if you dare.*

## METHOD

Chop the beans, tomatoes, apples, onions, garlic and ginger and put them into a large pan with the sugar, ground coriander and vinegar. Cook quickly for at least one hour, stirring regularly. When the chutney feels thick, add the green ginger

wine and lime juice. When the mixture is dangerously close to sticking to the pan, mix in the herbs and bottle straightaway. Keep for two weeks if possible before breaking it out, but it will still be great at the next bean harvest.

*Made at the height of the summer season when runner beans and green tomatoes are in plentiful supply, this cracking concoction will keep beautifully to give away as a Christmas present. Splendid in sandwiches, it adds bite and interest to smoked cheese or marmalade-glazed ham. Lovely with cold roast pork and boiled potatoes from the day before, sprinkled with sage and fried in a little olive oil. With a Scotch egg or salami salad, it's gorgeous green eating!*

Makes about seven 500g (1 lb) jars.

# QUICK CORIANDER RELISH

*A fast and furious, fiery relish with an aroma to tantalize the tastebuds.*

## INGREDIENTS

| | |
|---|---|
| 1 large bunch | Fresh coriander |
| 1 tbs | Shredded fresh ginger |
| 2 | Garlic cloves |
| 1 | Red onion, peeled |
| 3 | Green chillies |
| 1 tsp | Caster sugar |
| ½ tsp | Salt |
| Juice of 1 | Lime |
| 2 tbs | White wine vinegar |
| 1 tbs | Peanut or sesame oil |

## CHEF'S TIP

*Leave the chillies out if you prefer and replace them with a little extra onion. Add a few sprigs of fresh mint for a cooler relish. Add a tablespoon of peanut butter for a nuttier taste.*

## METHOD

For a smooth relish, simply liquidise all the ingredients to a paste. If you prefer it chunky, simply chop everything, then mix in the sugar, salt, lime juice, vinegar and oil. Either version can be served immediately or kept for up to two days in the fridge.

## USES

*The smooth version is especially versatile. I spread it on hot Naan bread, top it with grated Edam and grill it for a minute. Stunning! A fabulous dip with fresh vegetables, chapatis or mini-puris. Spread it on chicken legs or lamb kebabs and throw them on the barbecue. Use it to top a fillet steak just before it's finished cooking, sprinkle with brown sugar and caramelise under the grill - wickedly wonderful!*

*Fragrant and fiery, the chunky version is a great side dish with Thai or Indian food. Works wonders for chicken salad, plain quiche or tomato omelette. Try it with pizza and spoon it on to a pile of grated carrot.*

Makes about 175g (6 oz)

# PEPPERIFFIC RELISH

*A naturally sweet, colourful and appetising relish to pep up pasta or liven up a light lunch.*

| INGREDIENTS | |
|---|---|
| 1 | Red pepper |
| 1 | Yellow pepper |
| 1 | Orange pepper |
| | Olive oil |
| 1 tsp | Sea salt |
| ½ tsp | Ground black pepper |
| 2 | Red onions, peeled, topped and tailed |
| 6 | Garlic cloves |
| 3 sprigs | Fresh rosemary |
| 3 sprigs | Fresh thyme |
| 3 sprigs | Fresh basil |
| 1 tsp | Pink peppercorns |
| | Red wine vinegar |

## CHEF'S TIP

*Peel the peppers after roasting. When you have eaten all the pieces of relish, use the leftover liquid in salad dressings.*

Set the oven to medium heat. Halve and de-seed the peppers. Sprinkle olive oil, salt and pepper over the onions, garlic and insides of the peppers. Roast the whole onions for 15 minutes then add the peppers. Roast for 15 minutes more then add the garlic and roast everything for 10 minutes more. Peel the peppers, chop them with the onions and garlic and pile everything into wide-necked jars interspersed prettily with the herb sprigs and peppercorns. Fill halfway with red wine vinegar and top up with olive oil. Store for 3 days before using. Dig deep into the jar for the full range of flavours. Keeps for 2 months.

## USES

*Ideal as a relish with a generous slab of home-cooked pork terrine or gammon. Serve it on the side with a herb omelette. Build a salad of lollo rosso lettuce, fresh basil and coriander, pine nuts, spring onions and cherry tomatoes. Top with a good helping of Pepperiffic Relish, add a wedge of Dolcelatte and you'll feel like bursting into La Traviata. Staying Italian, pasta is a must with Pepperiffic. Try wholewheat or tricolour varieties and add a couple of sundried tomatoes or juicy black olives for an authentic touch.*

Makes about two 500g (1 lb) jars.

# STICKY PEACH CHUTNEY

*A ribsticker of a chutney, honeyed and fruity with the exotic flavours of nutmeg and cinnamon, coriander and ginger.*

## INGREDIENTS

| | |
|---|---|
| 15 | Peaches |
| 1 tbs | Mustard seeds |
| 3 tbs | Honey |
| 1 tbs | Ground ginger |
| 1 tbs | Cinnamon |
| 1 tbs | Ground coriander |
| 1 tbs | Nutmeg |
| 250g (8 oz) | Sultanas |
| 250g (8 oz) | Onions, chopped |
| 1 tsp | Salt |
| 1 tsp | White pepper |
| | Cider vinegar, to cover |

## CHEF'S TIP

*Use nectarines, mangoes or pawpaws if the price is right. This chutney is also delicious made with plums or greengages.*

## METHOD

Peel, stone and chop the peaches. Lightly crush the mustard seeds. Pile all the ingredients into a big pan or wok. Cover with the vinegar and cook for about two hours until the chutney 'draws' across the bottom of the pan. Stir well during cooking and add a little water if it starts to stick. Jar it hot and store for a month. Keeps at least a year.

## USES

*A cracker with curry or serve it at the start of an Indian meal with poppadoms, raita and carrot sticks. Dunk your chapatis in it during the meal. Sticky Peach is a marvellous partner for cheese, especially a good strong Cheddar. Makes an unusual sauce for deep fried Brie. Excellent with the contrasting saltiness of a good gammon steak. A great glaze on grilled lamb chops. Mix it with lemon juice and sesame oil and you'll discover a delicious dip for Thai titbits.*
Makes about five 500g (1 lb) jars.

# SUNBURST CHUTNEY

*Each jar contains a succulent selection of golden fruits and vegetables decorated with slices of sun. Original and different.*

## INGREDIENTS

| | |
|---|---|
| 10 | Seedless oranges |
| 125g (4 oz) | Dried apricots |
| 125g (4 oz) | Sultanas |
| 2 tsp | Coriander seeds, crushed |
| 1 small can | Pineapple chunks |
| 2 | Carrots, peeled and cut into strips |
| 2 | Onions, chopped |
| 1 | Yellow or orange pepper, deseeded and chopped |
| 600ml (1 pt) | White wine vinegar |
| 2 tsp | Salt |
| 250g (8 oz) | Caster sugar |

## METHOD

Squeeze the juice from three oranges and use it to soak the apricots and sultanas with the coriander seeds for two hours - or overnight for extra plumpness. Peel and rough-chop six oranges. Slice the remaining orange thinly - these are your sunbursts. Poach the fruit and vegetables with the coriander seeds, in just enough water to cover, for 30 minutes, stirring well. Add the vinegar, salt and sugar and bubble for a further hour till the chutney 'draws' across the pan. Use wide-necked jars, pressing a slice of orange against the glass as you spoon in the chutney until the sunburst is held in place. Ready now but will keep at least a year.

## USES

*Wonderful with honey-glazed ham or West Country farmhouse*

*Cheddar. Great as a ray of sunshine on a Ploughmans, with a pork steak or grilled lamb chops. Curries cry out for it. Tantalising with tandoori, brilliant with barbecued banquets. Grabs grilled fish by the gills and acts as an outstanding glaze for a gently roasting duck. It's so fruity, you can just pile it on to crusty bread and enjoy it as jam.*

Makes about four 500g (1 lb) jars.

# ZINGY LEMON CHUTNEY

*A zesty, vibrant chutney combining the tang of lemons with the rich taste of apricots and a crunch of apple.*

## INGREDIENTS

| | |
|---|---|
| 500g (1 lb) | Dried apricots |
| 600ml (1 pt) | Cider or apple juice |
| 500g (1 lb) | Apples, chopped |
| 500g (1 lb) | Onions, chopped |
| 4 | Lemons, zested and squeezed |
| 4 | Lemons, de-pipped and roughly chopped |
| 2 tsp | Salt |
| Walnut-sized piece | Fresh ginger in julienne strips |
| 1 tbs | Coriander seeds, crushed |
| 2 tbs | Honey |
| 600ml (1 pt) | Cider vinegar |
| 500g (1 lb) | Demerara sugar |

## METHOD

Soak the apricots for two hours in the apple juice or cider. Put all the ingredients into a large pan and bubble for 1½ hours, stirring well. When the chutney loses its foamy top and looks glossy, it's done. Ready now or will keep at least a year.

*Outstanding with Chicken Tikka or rice dishes like biriani. Excellent with minted lamb burgers and double-good as a glaze on gammon or duck. Poach a pork steak or chicken thighs in cider and add a tablespoonful of chutney plus the juice of half an orange to make a cracking, fat-free citrus sauce. Equally tasty with hoki or haddock instead of the meat. Take a tablespoonful, add a teaspoonful of sesame oil, a teaspoonful of light soy and a shake of Vicious Vinegar (page 43) for an interesting oriental dip - good with red pepper and cucumber sticks. Try it with a robust cheese. Mix a tablespoonful with an equal amount of raspberry vinegar as a different sauce for deep-fried Port Salut cheese.*

Makes about five 500g (1 lb) jars.

# BANGKOK BLASTER

*A fiery, tastebud-tingling Thai-style dressing. Sweet, nutty and ferocious. A visual delight - keep one as kitchen decoration.*

| INGREDIENTS | |
|---|---|
| 1 sprig | Coriander |
| 1 sprig | Rosemary |
| 1 sprig | Fennel |
| 1 sprig | Thyme |

| | |
|---|---|
| 2 | Garlic cloves |
| 1 long | Red chilli, split lengthways |
| 6 | Cashew nuts |
| 6 strips | Fresh ginger |
| 1 | Spring onion |
| | Peanut or sesame oil |
| | White wine vinegar |
| ½ tsp | Coriander seed |
| Pinch | Salt |
| Pinch | Garlic pepper |
| 2 tsp | Caster sugar or runny honey |
| ½ tsp | Dried red chillies, crushed |

## CHEF'S TIP

*Find yourself some unusual clear bottles. Tall, slim ones are especially useful to show off the herbs. Don't expose this dressing to strong sunlight as the greenery fades, but as it really is too pretty to hide away - make it, use it and make some more.*

Into each bottle, post the herb sprigs, garlic, chilli, cashew nuts, ginger and whole, trimmed spring onion. If it's a particularly long bottle, choose a stiff sprig of rosemary (or a satay skewer) and thread the chilli and garlic on to it before posting it into the bottle. This trick stops everything in the dressing floating to the top. Add the remaining ingredients in ratios to suit you, seal and give the bottle a good shake. The longer you leave the chilli in the dressing, the hotter it becomes. Keeps a year - or two.

*Try it on pancake rolls, Chinese dumplings, seafood, noodles, chicken, fish and crispy salads. Shakes up a stir-fry, wakes up a satay. Delicious with raw grated carrot, fresh ginger and strips of cucumber for an instant Thai relish with bite. Highly memorable in hot and sour soup.*

Makes a 250ml (8 fl oz) bottle.

# VICIOUS VINEGAR

*A volcanic vinegar to shock the most jaded palate into action.*

| | |
|---|---|
| 3 | Long red chillies |
| 6 | Garlic cloves |
| 1 tbs | Demerara sugar |
| 1 tsp | Salt |
| 1 tsp | Black peppercorns |
| 600ml (1 pt) | White wine vinegar |

Slice the chillies in half lengthwise, leaving the seeds inside. Peel the garlic. Thread the chillies on to a satay skewer, alternating with the garlic. Place the skewer in a tall, slim bottle, add the other ingredients and shake gently. You can also use a sturdy sprig of rosemary instead of the skewer, puncturing the garlic and chillies first for easy threading. A length of fennel stalk is also effective, particularly if you're a fan of aniseed flavours. Leave for two weeks for the flavours to develop or up to a year for the full viciousness.

## U S E S

*Makes a stunning sweet and sour sauce with pineapple, red pepper, muscovado sugar, a splash of soy sauce and orange juice. Whips up a wild salad dressing when mixed 50/50 with olive oil. Zings up soup. Turns chips into An Experience. Makes a ravishing relish when added to strips of cucumber or sliced shallots. For a zappy accompaniment to a Thai meal, pour over a small bowl of fresh mango.*

Makes about 600ml (1 pt).

# CITRUS SPECIAL

*This oil-free dressing will kickstart your tastebuds into action with a vengeance. Fruity, full of flavour and cholesterol-free.*

## I N G R E D I E N T S

| | |
|---|---|
| 1 Orange | Spiral peel and juice |
| 1 Lime | Spiral peel and juice |
| 1 Lemon | Spiral peel and juice |

| 4 tbs | Raspberry vinegar |
|-------|-------------------|
| 1 tbs | Coriander seeds, crushed |
| 1 tbs | Coarse-grain mustard |
| 1 tsp | Chives, chopped |
| 1 tsp | Thyme, chopped |
| 2 tbs | Honey or 2 tsp granulated sweetener |
| ½ tsp | Black pepper |
| Pinch | Salt |

## CHEF'S TIP

*Use a potato peeler to cut a peel spiral as long as possible from good quality, hard citrus fruits.*

## METHOD

Thread citrus peel spirals on to a wooden satay skewer. Insert the skewer into a tall bottle with a reasonably wide neck. Mix the remaining ingredients in a jug and fill the bottle with your fat-free, healthy mixture. Ready immediately or will keep for up to a month.

## USES

*Magnificent as a marinade or sauce for grilled chicken or white fish. Try soaking dried apricots or raisins in it and adding them to a bowl of grated carrot and ginger for a crunchy, cheerful dish. Adds zap to a green salad with celery and cashews and peps up kebabs of prawns with red pepper and onion. Try it over slices of grilled fresh pineapple. Peel and chop an orange or grapefruit, poach it in this dressing, thicken with extra honey and you'll have a fast and fruity sauce for duck, chicken, lamb or mackerel.*

Makes about 250ml (8 fl oz).

# DI MAGGIO

*A luxurious dressing or sauce redolent with the sunshine flavours of Italy's best produce.*

## INGREDIENTS

| | |
|---|---|
| 3 tbs | Tomato purée |
| 1 tsp | Basil |
| 1 tsp | Thyme |
| 1 tsp | Oregano |
| 1 tsp | Rosemary |
| 2 tbs | Honey |
| 1 tsp | Salt |
| 1 tsp | Black pepper |
| 1 tbs | Garlic, crushed |
| 125ml (4 fl oz) | Olive oil |
| 175ml (6 fl oz) | Red wine |
| 125ml (4 fl oz) | Red wine vinegar |

## METHOD

Using a large jug, mix together the tomato purée, herbs, honey, salt, pepper and garlic. Add the olive oil gradually, then the red wine and vinegar. Taste and adjust to suit your palate. Pour into bottles or jars. Will keep at its best for about 3 months.

## USES

*Give your table a taste of Tuscany by using this on a leafy salad with mozzarella and fresh basil. Serve with crab and pasta for a Mediterranean wave of flavours. Adds zest to tomato soup or vegetable casserole. Mash into Bel Paese cheese or Pesto for a smooth Italian-style dip. Spread it on crusty Ciabata bread, add fresh tomato slices and slivers of Dolcelatte. Add it to a pan of buttery shrimps, serve on a hot Naan bread and garnish with lemon slices and fresh coriander.*

Makes about 550ml (18 fl oz).

# LUCIFER'S SOUP

*A real devil's brew of a dressing with an oriental air. Warm and spicy, it makes a tantalising marinade, especially for pork.*

## INGREDIENTS

| | |
|---|---|
| 3 tbs | French mustard |
| 1 tbs | Ground ginger |
| ½ tsp | Cinnamon |
| 1 tbs | Honey |
| 2 tbs | Muscovado sugar |
| 1 tbs | Mustard seeds, crushed |
| 1 tsp | Ground black pepper |
| 1 tbs | Sesame oil |
| 1 tbs | Walnut oil |
| 300 ml (½ pt) | Cream sherry |
| 1 tbs | Light soy sauce |
| 300 ml (½ pt) | Malt vinegar |

## CHEF'S TIP

*Both sesame and walnut oil are strong flavoured and will overpower the rest of the ingredients if you use much more than the suggested amounts. Equally delicious if you leave the oil out altogether.*

## METHOD

Mix the mustard, ginger, cinnamon, honey, sugar, mustard seeds and pepper together in a big jug. Keep stirring and add the oils, sherry, soy sauce and vinegar. A devilish concoction will appear before your very eyes. It will keep a year, but bottle it before it grows horns and a pointy tail ...

## USES

*Marinate pork tenderloin overnight. Cook it fast in a hot oven the next day, basting with the Lucifer's. Slice thinly, serve wrapped in crispy Cos lettuce leaves and enjoy the distinctive flavour. Chicken enjoys it, too.* *Add a tablespoonful to a couple of carrots grated with a teaspoon of fresh ginger and a tablespoonful each of raisins and dried apricots and voila! - an unusual, fruity salad. For satay sauce, add a few sesame seeds and a tablespoonful of dressing to the same amount of crunchy peanut butter. Amazing on an avocado. Stunning poured over parsnips prior to roasting. Splash it into oxtail soup for a winter warmer with a sting in the tail.*

Makes about 600ml (1 pt).

# DRACULA'S DREAD

*A drop of this on your salad and the vampires will definitely leave you alone at night. Used as a mouthwatering marinade, it's a firm favourite with garlic maniacs.*

| INGREDIENTS | |
|---|---|
| 20 | Garlic cloves |
| 1 tbs | Garlic purée |
| 1 tsp | Garlic salt |
| 1 tsp | Ground black pepper |
| 2 | Onions |
| 1 | Leek, green and white parts or 4 spring onions |
| 1 tbs | Mustard seeds |
| 2 tbs | Caster sugar |
| 1 tsp | Mustard powder |
| 1 tbs | Mixed fresh herbs |
| 300ml (½ pt) | Olive oil |
| | White wine vinegar |

## CHEF'S TIP

*Wide-necked bottles or chunky jars are best for this thick dressing.*

## METHOD

Liquidise all the ingredients except the vinegar.
Make a thick purée then add the vinegar little by
little until you have the consistency you like. Adjust
the seasoning to suit. Omit either the oil *or* the
vinegar if you wish - it still tastes terrific. It will guard
you well for 2-3 months.

## USES

*Fabulous with fish or seafood, especially giant prawns or a firm fish
like hoki, grilled or barbecued. Marinate the fish and keep basting it
during cooking. Makes a cracking coleslaw. Mash it into a tub of
garlic cheese for a dracula-defying dip. Spread it on crusty French
bread. Perks up pasta a treat. Paint it on a roasting chicken or leg of
lamb and add it to the gravy - or layer leeks and parsnips in an
ovenproof dish, pour over some dressing and bake them with the roast.
Try with mashed potatoes or swede. Great on grilled tomatoes.*

Makes about 600ml (1 pt).

# VASSILIKI

*Drizzle this on your salad and close your eyes. Listen to that bouzouki music, waves lapping a white Ionian beach, cicadas in the fig trees ...*

## INGREDIENTS

Black or green olives
Garlic cloves
Strips of red pepper
Slices of fresh lemon
Sprigs of rosemary, thyme, oregano, basil, fennel
Olive oil
Runny honey
White wine vinegar
Sea salt

## CHEF'S TIP

*Add extra dried or fresh oregano if you like a really herby flavour.*

## METHOD

Post the olives, garlic and red pepper into bottles. Roll up the lemon slices and pop them in. Follow the lemon with the herb sprigs. Use a jug to mix the other ingredients to suit your taste, top up the bottles, seal, shake and serve.
Use immediately or will keep about 4 months.

*Excellent with a classic Greek salad. Chop tomatoes, cucumber, red onion, green peppers. Add Feta cheese and black olives, if you care for them. Serve with a basket of bread, Greek dips and lamb kebabs. A marvellous marinade for sardines, especially for barbecues. Adds a touch of genius to a consommé and complements a Cos lettuce for a simple summer salad. Try it on raw red cabbage with raisins and grated carrots for a healthy winter cruncher.*

Makes as much as you like.

# STARTLING SHERRY VINEGAR

*If you cherish classy condiments, here's one for you. Mouthwateringly marvellous with fruity overtones and a fleeting touch of fire.*

## INGREDIENTS

| | |
|---|---|
| 2 | Garlic cloves |
| 1 whole | Red chilli, split lengthways |
| 1 tbs | Fresh ginger shreds |
| 1 slice | Lime or lemon |
| 4 strips | Lime or lemon peel |
| 1 tsp | Mustard seeds |
| 1 tsp | Salt |
| 2 tsp | Caster sugar |
| 300ml (½ pt) | Sherry vinegar |

## CHEF'S TIP

*If you can't get sherry vinegar, mix white wine or cider*

*vinegar half and half with pale cream sherry.*

Post the garlic, chilli, ginger, lime or lemon slice and strips of peel into an elegant bottle. Add the mustard seeds, salt and sugar. Top up with the sherry vinegar, seal and shake. Leave to steep for a week or two before daring to try it. The heat factor will increase as time goes by. Keeps for at least a year.

*Opens the eyes of an oxtail soup. Delicious for dousing your pommes frites if you're dining out in diamonds and Dior. Adds tingle and bite to sautéed monkfish, prawn wontons or spring rolls. Tantalising with tomatoes. Just slice them thinly, crunch the pepper mill over them, add fresh sorrel or basil leaves and trickle on the vinegar. Soak cucumber strips for a couple of hours for a divine side dish for Thai food. Carrots are equally grateful for this treatment and if you add sliced oranges and crushed coriander seeds to the carrots, even better.*

Makes about 350ml (12 fl oz)

# OLD ENGLISH DRESSING

*As an alternative to French dressing, try Old English. Oil free, but full of flavour, it needs English lettuce, English cucumber and English tomatoes for a tasty traditional salad.*

| | |
|---|---|
| 1 tbs | English mustard |
| 1 tbs | Tomato purée |
| 1 tbs | Honey |

| | |
|---|---|
| 1 tbs | Shallot, finely chopped |
| 1 tbs | Mustard seeds |
| 1 tbs | Fresh thyme, chopped |
| ½ tsp | Salt |
| ½ tsp | Black pepper |
| 150ml (¼ pt) | Sherry |
| 600ml (1 pt) | Cider vinegar |

## CHEF'S TIP

*If you must have oil in your dressing, try walnut oil for a distinguished flavour.*

## METHOD

Mix all the ingredients (except the sherry and vinegar) to a smooth purée, then add the sherry and vinegar until you have the consistency and alcohol level you desire. Use straightaway if you wish. Bottle it and it will keep three months.

## USES

*Try over Little Gem or Buttercrunch lettuce hearts, celery, peeled cucumber (fresh out of the greenhouse, if possible) and spring onions from the garden as a great green salad with grilled fish, crêpes or fried chicken. A bowl of grated carrot and a handful of sultanas benefit from a tablespoonful of this dressing. Mixed with Hollandaise sauce or Greek yogurt, it makes a delicious devilled dip. Add it to baked beans for a bit of zap. As a dressing over thinly sliced cold, rare roast beef, it's a dream. Marinate steak or chicken kebabs in it overnight and grill them for lunch.*

Makes about 800ml
(27 fl oz).

# RED DRAGON

*An oriental dressing with a touch of mystery and a discreet sting in the tail.*

## INGREDIENTS

| | |
|---|---|
| 1 | Cinnamon stick |
| 1 slice | Orange |
| 300ml (½ pt) | Red wine vinegar or Chinese red vinegar |
| 1 tsp | Sesame oil |
| 2 tsp | Light soy sauce |
| 2 tsp | Honey |
| ½ tsp | Black pepper |
| ½ tsp | Mustard seeds |
| ½ tsp | Szechuan peppercorns |
| 1 | Dried red chilli, crumbled |
| 1 | Spring onion, chopped |
| 1 tsp | Fresh ginger, finely chopped |

## CHEF'S TIP

*Use soya oil instead of sesame or leave it out altogether if you prefer. Replace the honey with granulated sweetener if you're slimming.*

## METHOD

Post the cinnamon stick and orange slice (roll it up, it's easier) into a long decorative bottle. Add the remaining ingredients. Leave to steep for a week then unscrew the lid and breathe in those tempting aromas ... If you can resist, it will keep for at least a year.

## USES

*Shred some Chinese leaf into a bowl, add a chopped spring onion, strips of cucumber and a tablespoonful of dressing for a great accompaniment to a meal full of Eastern promise. Stunning with spring rolls or prawn wontons. Breathes fire into hot and sour soup, fights fattiness in spare ribs and spikes up sweet and sour. Pickle a selection of chopped raw vegetables in it overnight - red pepper, raw parsnip, bamboo shoots, onion, white cabbage, carrot. Add 2 tablespoonfuls of dressing to a pan of poaching plums (no stones please), liquidise and you have a superb sauce for crispy roast duck.*

Makes about 325ml (11 fl oz)

# MINTY MUSTARD

*A piquant, aromatic dressing combining mint's cool appeal with the sweetness of honey and warmth of mustard. Ideal with avocado.*

| INGREDIENTS | |
|---|---|
| 1 tbs | Mustard seeds |
| 2 tbs | Mint jelly |
| 1 tbs | English mustard, ready-made |

| | |
|---|---|
| 2 tbs | Honey |
| 2 tbs | Fresh mint, chopped |
| 1 tsp | Garlic, crushed |
| 1 tsp | Salt |
| 1 tsp | Black pepper |
| 300ml (½ pt) | Olive oil |
| 600ml (1 pt) | Cider vinegar |

## CHEF'S TIP

*Use dried mint if you're really stuck. Fresh is better. It's easy to grow, but invasive, so plant it in a tub by the door. Try replacing mint jelly with redcurrant jelly. This dressing is delicious made with raspberry or red wine vinegar for a change.*

## METHOD

In a large jug, mash together the mustard seeds, mint jelly, English mustard, honey, mint, garlic, salt and pepper. Mix in the olive oil, then the vinegar. Decant into bottles. Can be served immediately. Keeps for at least 6 months.

## USES

*A meltingly marvellous marinade, luscious with lamb, fabulous with fish and cheeky with chicken. Turns a Chinese leaf and cucumber combination into an experience. Try it on a warm salad of lightly poached carrot and swede shreds. Pour it over a plate of thinly sliced tomatoes for a memorable side dish. Add it to a carton of natural yogurt for a piquant dip with Greek or Indian food. For perfect potatoes to serve with lamb, smear an ovenproof dish with olive oil, add thinly sliced potatoes and a handful of chopped shallots, then drizzle with dressing. Bake with the lamb until crispy on top. Wonderful ...*

Makes about 1 litre (1¾ pt).

# Embarrassed Eggs

*If you like food with attitude, you'll love these blushing babies!*

| | |
|---|---|
| 1 dozen | Hard-boiled eggs |
| 1 | Red onion |
| 1 stick | Celery |
| 3 sprigs | Rosemary |
| $\frac{1}{4}$ tsp | Chilli seasoning |
| $\frac{1}{2}$ tsp | Caster sugar |
| $\frac{1}{2}$ tsp | Black pepper |
| $\frac{1}{2}$ tsp | Mustard seeds |
| 1 tsp | Light soy sauce |
| | Beetroot vinegar |

*To make beetroot vinegar, stand two baby beets in distilled malt vinegar overnight to impart a rich red shade. Eat the beetroot, save the vinegar.*

## METHOD

Peel the eggs carefully and stand them in fresh cold water. Don't use any eggs if the yolk is exposed or the vinegar will be cloudy and unappealing - mash them up for sandwiches instead. Slice the red onion, leaving the slices whole. Chop the celery. Put three eggs into a wide-necked jar then a sprinkling of celery. Push the onion slices and rosemary against the glass for decorative effect. Hold them in place with the next layer of eggs and celery. Continue until the jar is full, sprinkle on the seasonings and pour in the vinegar. Leave two weeks before using to allow a distinct blush to develop. Will keep for six months.

## USES

*An interesting addition to a salad at any time of year. Popular with a Ploughmans, especially with a slab of farmhouse Cheddar and a wedge of Melton Mowbray pork pie. Add tomatoes fresh from the garden, crunchy pickled onions and crusty bread and the neighbours will be queueing down your garden path to invite themselves to lunch. Serve Embarrassed Eggs with pickled red cabbage and beetroot as a 'Pink Pickle Platter' - but provide bibs!*

Makes 12.

# EXPLOSIVE EGGS

*These little beasties will completely blather the back of your throat. Hot and spicy - pickled eggs like you've never tasted before.*

## INGREDIENTS

| | |
|---|---|
| 1 dozen | Hard-boiled eggs |
| 3 cloves | Garlic, peeled and sliced |
| 3 | Long red chillies, sliced diagonally |
| 1 tsp | Crushed dried red chillies |
| 1 tsp | Mustard seeds |
| 1 tsp | Salt |
| 1 tsp | Coarsely ground black pepper |
| 1 tsp | Caster sugar |
| | Distilled white vinegar |

## CHEF'S TIP

*Add a few sprigs of curry herb or marjoram to the jar for decorative effect.*

## METHOD

Layer the eggs gently in a wide-necked jar with the garlic and sliced chillies. Add the crushed dried chillies, spices, seasonings and sugar then pour in the vinegar. Store for a month before using - then stand by for lift-off. They will keep in this stratosphere for about six months.

## USES

*Great in a bag of cheese and onion crisps with a sprinkling of Worcestershire Sauce for 'egg and chips'. Add a salami stick for 'sausage, egg and chips'. Wash the feast down with a pint of ale over a game of darts or dominoes.*

Makes 12.

# TRADITIONAL PICKLED EGGS

*Mild and mellow, these eggs are chilli-free, garlic-free and herb-free for those who like plain, wholesome fare.*

## INGREDIENTS

| | |
|---|---|
| 1 dozen | Hard-boiled eggs |
| 4 small | Celery sticks, complete with leaf |
| 1 tsp | Salt |
| 1 tsp | Black peppercorns |
| 1 tsp | Caster sugar |
| | Cider vinegar |

## CHEF'S TIP

*Try substituting quail, duck, goose or pheasant eggs.*

## METHOD

Peel and rinse the eggs carefully and slide them gently into a wide-necked jar, pushing the celery on to the glass for decoration. Add the salt, peppercorns and sugar, then top up with vinegar, making sure all the eggs are covered. Store for a fortnight before breaking open. Will keep at least six months.

## USES

*This is the type of fare to bring out when a bunch of lads are settling down in front of the football on TV. Crack open the crisps, crusty French bread, cheese, pork pies, hot sausages, Heartstarter pickled onions (page 65) and these Traditional Pickled Eggs. Sling in a six-pack of beers, open the windows and go away for the rest of the weekend.*

Makes 12.

# GARLIC MANIACS

*If you're seriously into garlic, you'll adore these pickled onions, packed with garlic, garlic and extra garlic.*

## INGREDIENTS

| | |
|---|---|
| 500g (1 lb) | Pickling onions |
| 1 tsp | Garlic salt |
| 1 tsp | Black pepper |
| 10 cloves | Garlic, whole |
| 10 cloves | Garlic, sliced |
| 1 tbs | Caster sugar |
| | White wine vinegar or |
| | distilled white malt vinegar |
| 4 sprigs | Oregano |
| 4 sprigs | Marjoram |
| 2 slices | Lemon |

## CHEF'S TIP

*These onions may develop a turquoise hue. Strange, but true. It's a personality trait of garlic and it's quite normal. Go ahead and eat! Garlic is easy to grow. Dig a patch of garden in Autumn. Pop in a row of garlic cloves, pointed end up. Harvest in August.*

## METHOD

Stack the onions into jars, interspersing them with the garlic. Press the herb sprigs and lemon slices against the inside of the glass and hold them in place with onions. Add the seasonings and sugar. Top up with vinegar. Add a sliced red chilli for heat, or triangles of red pepper for extra colour. Store in a dark place for up to a year but a minimum of a month will develop a flavour fit for garlic maniacs.

*Eat one of these and everyone must eat one. I know people who finish the onions then drain the jar for the garlic cloves and eat them as well. Pickled garlic is very tasty - mild and sweet if you use this recipe. Outstanding sliced up, fried to a crisp and served tossed in Singapore*

noodles with peanuts and shredded basil. *Terrific baked round a leg of pork or added to the stuffing for a chicken. Serve them in a tomato, mozzarella and basil salad as a side dish for lasagne.*

Makes about two 500g (1 lb) jars.

# DELHI DARLINGS

*Evoke the subtle aromas and flavours of Kashmir and Madras with these delicious spiced onions - redolent with cardamom, cumin, coriander ...*

## INGREDIENTS

| | |
|---|---|
| 500g (1 lb) | Pickling onions, peeled |
| 1 tsp | Cloves |
| 1 tsp | Cardamom pods |
| 1 tsp | Coriander seeds |
| 1 tsp | Cumin |
| 1 tsp | Mustard seeds |
| 1 tsp | Black peppercorns |
| 1 | Cinnamon stick |
| 1 tsp | Salt |
| 4 tsp | Dark brown sugar |
| | Pickling vinegar |

## CHEF'S TIP

*Use a small sharp knife, rather than your fingernails, to peel the onions. Working by an open door or window - better still, sitting in the garden if the weather allows - will alleviate the streaming eyes syndrome. The best solution of all is to wear contact lenses!*

## METHOD

Pack the onions into clean jars. Add the spices, salt and sugar. Top up with vinegar until all the onions are covered and screw the tops on tightly.  Store in a dark place for a month to allow the flavours to develop - and no pinching one before the month is up!  Will keep at least a year.

### USES

*A Ploughman's lunch takes on a taste of the East when served with these.  Their sweet spiciness complements the great English cheeses; Cheddar, Stilton, Wensleydale and Cheshire.  Add a few to a casserole for a spiced piquancy and original flair.*

Makes about two 500g (1 lb) jars.

# MELLOW SYDS

*Mild but flavoursome, these onions are named after our friend Syd Arnold who says he's married to the only 'hot stuff' he likes!*

### INGREDIENTS

| | |
|---|---|
| 500g (1 lb) | Pickling onions, peeled |
| 1 tsp | Green or black peppercorns |
| 1 tsp | Coriander seeds |
| 1 tsp | Salt |
| 2 tbs | Muscovado sugar |
| | Malt vinegar |

### METHOD

Put everything in a big jar and leave it for a month.  An ideal gift for friends who don't like their food too spicy.  Cider vinegar can be substituted for the malt for an even milder flavour.  Will store for at least a year.

### USES

*Perfect for a picnic, a Ploughmans or a paté platter.*

Makes about two 500g (1 lb) jars.

# HEARTSTARTERS

*Not recommended for those of a nervous disposition. These onions will bump-start your cardiac system and decoke your arteries!*

## INGREDIENTS

| | |
|---|---|
| 500g (1 lb) | Pickling onions |
| 6 sprigs | Fresh rosemary and thyme |
| 8 | Long red chillies, split lengthways, seeds included |
| 1 tbs | Red pepper cubes |
| 1 tbs | Fresh ginger, sliced |
| 2 cloves | Garlic |
| 1 tsp | Salt |
| 1 tsp | Mustard seeds |
| 2 tbs | Demerara sugar |
| | Malt vinegar |

## CHEF'S TIP

*You can use green chillies and peppers instead of red, but they tend to lose their colour. Red stays bright.*

## METHOD

Fill some interesting clear glass jars with the onions, pressing the herbs, chillies, red pepper pieces, ginger and garlic against the glass for visual interest. Add the salt, mustard seeds and sugar.

Top up with vinegar until all the onions are covered. Store for a month before trying - if you can stand the wait. Will keep for a good year.

Break out the cheeseboard. Try something different, perhaps low-fat mature Cheddar, Roquefort or fresh Parmesan. When you've consumed all these onions, keep the vinegar and just pop in some fresh picklers. Leave for another month and away you go again.

Makes about two 500g (1 lb) jars.

# ORIENTALS

Crisp little onions, redolent with the warmth and spiciness of the Orient. Extra healthy if made sugar-free .

**INGREDIENTS**

| | |
|---|---|
| 500g (1 lb) | Pickling onions, peeled |
| 3 cloves | Garlic |
| 1 tbs | Fresh ginger, chopped |
| 1 | Cinnamon stick |
| 3 'stars' | Star anise or 1 tsp |
| | Chinese seasoning |
| 1 | Red chilli, sliced |
| 1 tbs | Caster sugar |
| 1 tsp | Black peppercorns |
| 1 tbs | Soy sauce |
| 1 tsp | Sesame seeds, crushed |
| 2 tbs | Sherry |
| | White wine vinegar |

**CHEF'S TIP**

Substitute carrot strips for the onions for an interesting Oriental pickle.

**METHOD**

Pile the onions into jars, adding the garlic, ginger, cinnamon, star anise and chilli at the same time. Spoon in the sugar, peppercorns, soy sauce, sesame seeds and sherry. Top up with vinegar and leave to ferment for a month. Wonderful for a good year or so.

*Slicing these onions and adding them to a stir-fry or sweet and sour sauce adds an unusual dimension. Excellent quartered and served cold as a side-dish with Chinese starters like sesame prawn toasts, spare ribs or seaweed, counteracting rich flavours with ease. Use the vinegar as a dip - it's full of Eastern promise.*

Makes about two 500g (1 lb) jars.

# RED DEVILS

*Only for those who munch chillies for a hobby. These onions are guaranteed to clear a cold, a hangover and a room!*

## INGREDIENTS

| | |
|---|---|
| 500g (1 lb) | Pickling onions, peeled |
| 10 | West Indian wrinkled chillies (Granny's Bonnets) |
| 10 | Dried red chillies, whole |
| 1 tbs | Caster sugar |
| 1 tbs | Sea salt |
| 1 tbs | Pink peppercorns |
| | Distilled white malt vinegar |

## METHOD

Slice the fresh chillies. Pack the onions into jars interleaved with chillies, fresh and dried. Sprinkle in the sugar, salt and peppercorns and top up with vinegar. Leave for a month, but will fester evilly for a year.

## USES

*These will take your mind off a headache and, possibly, the enamel off*

your teeth. *I recommend fresh crusty bread to deaden the firepower a bit and a chunk of the strongest cheese your tongue can handle. Good luck.*

Makes about two 500g (1 lb) jars.

# HERBIES

*Herb-garden flavours complement crispy onions in this classic tracklement.*

## INGREDIENTS

| | |
|---|---|
| 500g (1 lb) | Pickling onions, peeled |
| Assorted sprigs | Rosemary, thyme, fennel, sage, parsley, lovage |
| 1 tbs | Muscovado sugar |
| 1 tbs | Salt |
| 1 tbs | Pink peppercorns |
| 1 tbs | Pickling spice |
| | Cider vinegar |

## CHEF'S TIP

*These onions look great made with distilled white malt vinegar - in which case use caster sugar, no sugar or 1 teaspoonful of granulated sweetener. For fruitiness, add chunks of dessert apple or a tablespoonful of sultanas.*

## METHOD

Stack the onions into clean jars, scattering the herb sprigs, sugar, salt and spices among them. Top up generously with vinegar and keep for a month before tucking in. Will store for a year or so.

## USES

*Perfect for anyone who loves pickled onions but doesn't like them too hot. Grans and children always go for these. Naturally, they complement good English cheeses - try Wensleydale, Blue Cheshire or Sage Derby for a change. Thread them on kebabs with Bratwurst for a tangy treat.*

Makes about two 500g (1 lb) jars.

# AFTERBURNERS

*Start the countdown now - these onions are rocket-launchingly hot.*

## INGREDIENTS

| | |
|---|---|
| 500g (1 lb) | Pickling onions, peeled |
| 1 tbs | Fresh ginger, sliced |
| 5 | West Indian wrinkled chillies (Granny's Bonnets) |
| 1 tbs | Curry powder |
| 1 tbs | Crushed dried red chillies |
| 1 tbs | Mustard seeds, crushed |
| 1 tbs | Honey |
| 1 tbs | Salt |
| | Malt vinegar |

## METHOD

Pile the onions into jars, interspersed with the ginger and West Indian chillies. Spoon in the curry powder, dried chillies and mustard seed. Mix the honey and salt with the vinegar and pour over the onions. They like six weeks to develop their full firepower, but will keep at least a year.

## USES

*Select a wedge of strong cheese and a baguette as long as your arm, add a fireproof dish of Afterburners and put NASA on stand-by.*

Makes about two 500g (1 lb) jars.

# CRANIUM CRUSHERS

*Sugar-free, brain-batteringly hot and crushingly crunchy.*

## INGREDIENTS

| | |
|---|---|
| 500g (1 lb) | Pickling onions, peeled |
| 10 | Long red chillies, split lengthways |
| 1 tsp | Salt |
| 1 tsp | Szechuan peppercorns |
| 1 tsp | Coriander seeds |
| | Malt vinegar |

## CHEF'S TIP

*Using cold vinegar is perfectly satisfactory - no need to boil it.*

## METHOD

Rinse the peeled onions. I never brine or soak them. Stack the onions into jars, interspersed with the chillies. Add the spices, then the vinegar, slowly so that the spices trickle down through the onions, lodging where they like, adding to the visual effect. Leave these onions for at least a month to gain the right pain level. The longer you leave them - a year is fine - the more mind-blowing they'll become. If you wish, remove the chillies when they're hot enough for you.

## USES

*These onions are ideal for that fellow who says 'Can't you make this any hotter?' when he's eating Vindaloo. To cure a cold or a hangover, take your life in your hands with half a dozen of these. Have a fire extinguisher handy. Believe it or not, I know people who eat the onions, then eat the chillies ...*

Makes about two 500g (1 lb) jars.

# RED HOT MAMAS

*Darkly delicious and distinctly incendiary.*

## INGREDIENTS

| | |
|---|---|
| 1 tbs | Runny honey |
| 1 tsp | Dark soy sauce |
| 1 tsp | Worcestershire sauce |
| 1 tbs | Muscovado sugar |
| | Malt vinegar |
| 500g (1 lb) | Pickling onions, peeled |
| 4 sprigs | Thyme |
| 2 tsp | Mustard seeds |
| 2 tsp | Black peppercorns |
| 1 tbs | Crushed dried red chillies |

## CHEF'S TIP

*Bruise the mustard seeds and peppercorns in a pestle and mortar to release their heat.*

## METHOD

Shake up the runny honey, soy sauce, Worcestershire sauce and sugar in a large jar with a good slosh of vinegar. Add the onions, interleaved with thyme sprigs and sprinklings of the crushed mustard seeds and peppercorns. Add the chillies and pour in sufficient vinegar to cover the onions completely. After a couple of days the vinegar will need topping up because the dried chillies and spices will have drunk some. Store in a cool place for six weeks.

## USES

*Brilliant with cold pork or gammon, especially with hot Jersey Royals. When you've finished the onions, add fresh onion slices, shredded carrots or white cabbage to the remaining vinegar.*

Makes about two 500g (1 lb) jars.

# SWEET AND SPICY

*Succulent sweet onions with spiced warmth, but not the firepower of chilli.*

## INGREDIENTS

| | |
|---|---|
| 500g (1 lb) | Pickling onions, peeled |
| 1 tsp | Soy sauce |
| 1 tsp | Coriander seeds, crushed |
| 1 tsp | Nutmeg |
| 1 tsp | Cinnamon |
| 1 tsp | Cardamom pods, crushed |
| ½ tsp | Mace |
| 1 tsp | Sultanas or raisins |
| 2 tbs | Muscovado sugar |
| 1 tsp | Black peppercorns, crushed |
| | Cider vinegar |

## CHEF'S TIP

*If you like a bit of extra heat, add a teaspoon of crushed mustard seeds.*

## METHOD

Pile the onions into jars with well-sealing lids. Spoon in the soy sauce, spices, sultanas, sugar and seasonings. Top up with vinegar. Leave for a month to allow those delicious, tantalising flavours to mature. Will keep for at least a year.

## USES

*I always think of Christmas cake when I'm making these onions. It's the enticing aroma of the spices that does it. On a freezing, foggy day in mid-November, peeling onions in a warm, spice-scented kitchen isn't so bad. These onions are brilliant with boiled ham for a simple supper. Try baking a few in a small ovenproof dish alongside the turkey for half an hour - definitely different.*

Makes about two 500g (1 lb) jars.

# Sweet Little Pinkies

*Pretty, petite, port-soaked, pink onions, particularly pleasing with a perfect Ploughmans.*

## INGREDIENTS

| | |
|---|---|
| 500g (1 lb) | Small pickling or silverskin onions |
| 3 tbs | Port |
| 2 tbs | Honey |
| 1 tbs | Caster sugar |
| 1 tsp | Sea salt |
| ½ tsp | Ground black pepper |
| ½ tsp | Grated nutmeg |
| | Red wine vinegar |

## CHEF'S TIP

*Try replacing the nutmeg with an inch of cinnamon stick or half a teaspoon of cardamom pods - or both.*

## METHOD

Fill an attractive jar or jars with the onions. Mix the remaining ingredients in a jug until the sugar dissolves and add to the onions, making sure they're all covered. Screw the lids on tight and store in a dark place for three weeks.

## USES

*Interesting poached in butter and brown sugar and served as hot toffee onions, especially with a gammon steak. Thread them on a kebab with mushrooms. Try Scotch Megs: take one Sweet Little Pinkie, wrap it in a strip of bacon, tuck it inside a stoned fresh apricot and encase that in sausagemeat. Roll in sage and onion suffing mix and bake with roast pork or turkey.*

Makes about two 500g (1 lb) jars.

# BBQ SAUCE

*Warm but not excessively hot, this sauce is studded with fruity flavours to complement any barbecued or grilled goodies - and it's oil-free.*

## INGREDIENTS

| | |
|---|---|
| 500g (1 lb) | Tomatoes |
| 125g (4 oz) | Dried apricots |
| 50g  (2 oz) | Sultanas |
| 50g  (2 oz) | Raisins |
| 2 | Onions, chopped |
| 1 | Apple, chopped |
| 4 | Garlic cloves |
| 2 | Red chillies |
| 125g (4 oz) | Pineapple |
| Juice of 1 | Orange |
| 1 tsp | Salt |
| 1 tsp | Black pepper |
| 2 tbs | Tomato purée |
| 300ml (½ pt) | Red wine vinegar |
| 150ml (¼ pt) | Sherry |
| 3 tbs | Brown sugar |
| 1 tbs | Mustard |
| Dash | Worcestershire sauce |

## CHEF'S TIP

*Soak the apricots, sultanas and raisins overnight in the sherry or they make the liquidizer 'cough'. Use fresh tomatoes if possible.*

## METHOD

Liquidize the tomatoes, apricots, sultanas, raisins, onions, apple, garlic, chillies and pineapple with the orange juice.  Pour the mixture into a large pan, add the remaining ingredients and bubble for 40 minutes,

stirring frequently, until you have a fragrant,
appetising delight. Bottle whatever you don't eat the
minute it's ready. Will keep for three months.

## USES

*Daub it all over sausages, burgers, spare ribs, duck breasts, steak or
kebabs during cooking. Superb spooned into a jacket potato.
Different as a dip with raw cauliflower florets and carrot sticks.
Spread it on French bread, top with sliced mushrooms and cheese and
pop the whole lot under the grill. Use it as a pizza base or serve it
with a prawn omelette. Wonderful in winter with tortilla chips as an
instant reminder of summer.*

Makes about 1.8 litres (3 pt).

# SWEARBOX SAMBAL

*A stunning relish, chock-full of chillies and laced with ginger and
garlic, this recipe pays homage to its Indonesian origins. Take your
first taste standing near a charity swearbox, money at the ready ...!*

## INGREDIENTS

| | |
|---|---|
| 1 kg (2 lb) | Tomatoes |
| 250g (8 oz) | Onions, chopped |
| 20 | Garlic cloves |
| Walnut-sized piece | Fresh ginger, peeled and chopped |
| 10 | Dried red chillies, crushed |
| 10 | Fresh red chillies, chopped, seeds included |
| Handful | Mixed fresh herbs *or* |
| 2 tsp | Mixed dried herbs |
| 2 tsp | Curry powder |
| 2 tsp | Chilli powder |

| 2 tsp | English mustard powder |
| 250g (8 oz) | Demerara sugar |
| 2 tsp | Worcestershire sauce |
| 4 tsp | Tomato purée |
| 300ml ($\frac{1}{2}$ pt) | Malt vinegar |
| 1 tsp | Garlic salt |
| 1 tsp | Black pepper |

## CHEF'S TIP

*Reduce the amount of chillies and mustard powder to suit you.*
*Equally delicious made chilli-free, resulting in a tasty tomato treat.*

## METHOD

Whizz the tomatoes, onions, garlic, ginger and chillies
in the liquidiser. Pour the mixture into a large pan.
Add the remaining ingredients (unless you are using
fresh herbs which I add 10 minutes before the end of
cooking time). Bubble for 45 minutes to thicken to a
purée. Bottle while it's still hot. Ready now. Keeps
for at least a year.

## USES

*An excellent tomato base for pepperoni pizza. For a sensational*
*savoury snack, toast a slice of bread, spread it with sambal, top with*
*Jarlsberg cheese, grill and eat. Swearbox is an excellent dip for*
*oriental food, especially satays or prawn toasts. Tasty with crudités,*
*particularly baby corn cobs. Superb with poached scallops. Add a*
*teaspoonful to your favourite salad dressing. Mix it with mayonnaise*
*as a dip for seafood. Makes a memorable marinade combined with*
*one tablespoonful each of olive oil and red wine.*

Makes about 1.5 litres ($2\frac{1}{2}$ pt).

# TANGY TOM

*Sugar-free, oil-free, multipurpose and savoury, ideal to make with your home-grown tomato harvest.*

## INGREDIENTS

| | |
|---|---|
| 1 kg (2 lb) | Tomatoes |
| 250g (8 oz) | Pickled gherkins |
| 4 large | Onions |
| 6 | Garlic cloves |
| Juice of 1 | Orange |
| Juice of 1 | Lemon |
| 1 carton | Passata |
| 2 tsp | Worcestershire sauce |
| 2 tsp | Fresh oregano |
| 2 tsp | Fresh thyme |
| 1 tsp | Salt |
| 1 tsp | Black pepper |
| 600ml (1 pt) | Distilled white malt vinegar |

## CHEF'S TIP

*Use tinned tomatoes if necessary. If you can't cope with sugar-free, add 250g (8 oz) caster sugar - but do try it without. If diet dictates that you omit the salt, replace it with a teaspoon of sage.*

## METHOD

Liquidize the tomatoes, skins and all, with the gherkins, onions and garlic. Pour the mixture into a large pan, adding the remaining ingredients. Cook for about 45 minutes, stirring frequently until you have a thick purée. Bottle and store in a dark place. Ready to use immediately. Develops in flavour if left a month. Keeps for a year.

*The perfect pasta partner - quick and quite delicious. Livens up a mixed grill, a cold collation or a herb and onion omelette. Spikes up a soup and makes a tasty pizza topping. Serve it as a calorie-conscious dip with celery sticks or mix it with fat-free mayonnaise, natural yogurt or low-fat cottage cheese for a hardly-naughty-at-all savoury dunk - marvellous with raw parsnip sticks! Lavish it on lamb cutlets for the barbecue or add a generous dollop to a bowlful of chilli. Introduce a tablespoonful to a stir-fry of courgettes and garlic - they'll be friends for life. Children love it with chicken nuggets or fish fingers. Of you can simply heat it and serve as a pour-over sauce with ribs or steaks. Versatile? Very!*

Makes about 1.5 litres (2½ pt).